SLITHERING SNAKES
Black Mambas
by Joanne Mattern
BLASTOFF! READERS
2
BELLWETHER MEDIA • MINNEAPOLIS, MN

Blastoff! Readers are carefully developed by literacy experts to build reading stamina and move students toward fluency by combining standards-based content with developmentally appropriate text.

Level 1 provides the most support through repetition of high-frequency words, light text, predictable sentence patterns, and strong visual support.

Level 2 offers early readers a bit more challenge through varied sentences, increased text load, and text-supportive special features.

Level 3 advances early-fluent readers toward fluency through increased text load, less reliance on photos, advancing concepts, longer sentences, and more complex special features.

★ **Blastoff! Universe**

Reading Level

Grade K

Grades 1–3

Grade 4

This edition first published in 2025 by Bellwether Media, Inc.

Library of Congress Cataloging-in-Publication Data

Names: Mattern, Joanne, 1963- author.
Title: Black mambas / by Joanne Mattern.
Description: Minneapolis, MN : Bellwether Media, Inc., 2025. | Series: Blastoff! readers: slithering snakes | Includes bibliographical references and index. | Audience: Ages 5-8 | Audience: Grades K-1 | Summary: "Simple text and full-color photography introduce beginning readers to black mambas. Developed by literacy experts for students in kindergarten through third grade"-- Provided by publisher.
Identifiers: LCCN 2024003113 (print) | LCCN 2024003114 (ebook) | ISBN 9798886870367 (library binding) | ISBN 9781644878804 (ebook)
Subjects: LCSH: Black mamba--Juvenile literature.
Classification: LCC QL666.O64 M377 2025 (print) | LCC QL666.O64 (ebook) | DDC 597.96/42--dc23/eng/20240208
LC record available at https://lccn.loc.gov/2024003113
LC ebook record available at https://lccn.loc.gov/2024003114

Editor: Betsy Rathburn Designer: Brittany McIntosh

Printed in the United States of America, North Mankato, MN.

Table of Contents

Danger!

Black mambas are among the most dangerous **reptiles** in the world. Their **venom** is deadly!

They live in many countries in Africa.

Black mambas are big snakes. They can be up to 14 feet (4.3 meters) long!

They weigh around 3.5 pounds (1.6 kilograms).

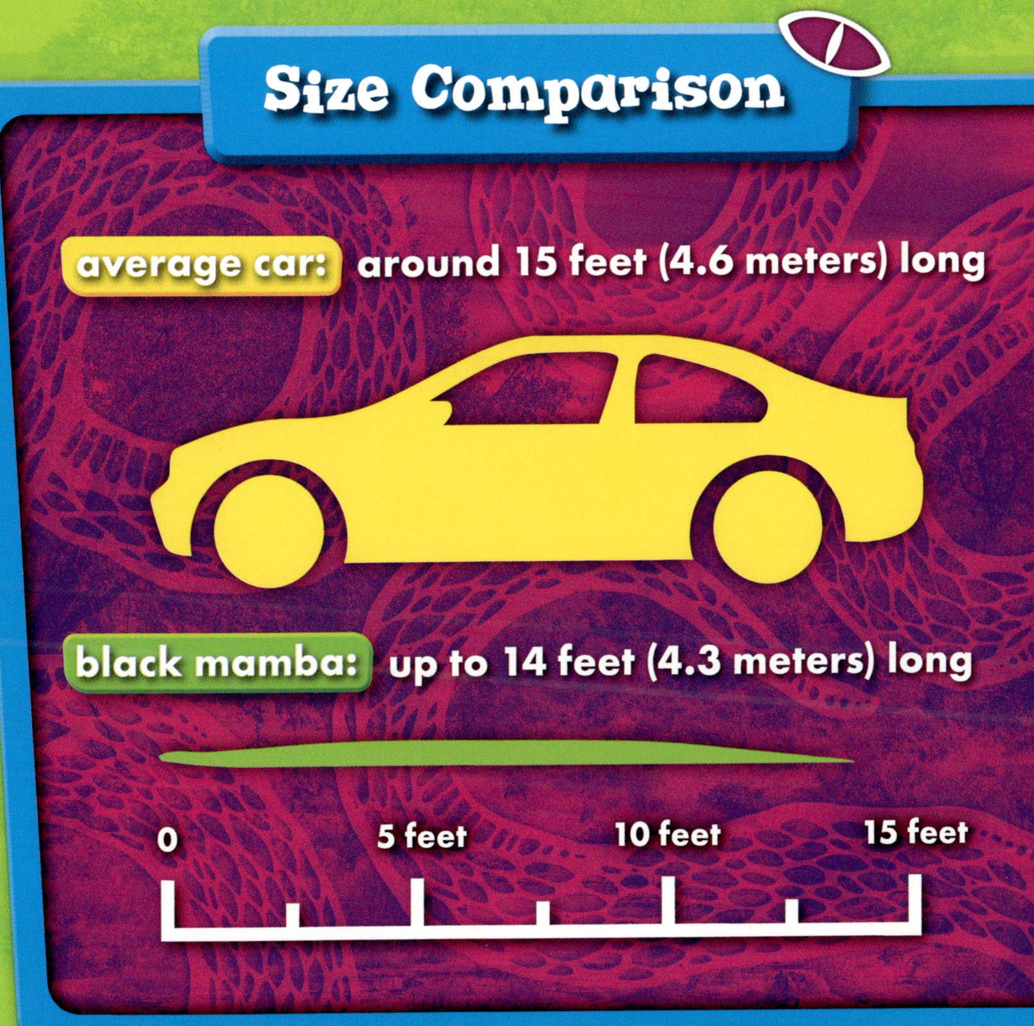

Black mambas have gray or brown **scales**.

The insides of their mouths are black. This is how they got their name!

Spot a Black Mamba!

On the Hunt

Black mambas live in forests and rocky **savannas**.

They are active during the day. They often **bask** to keep warm.

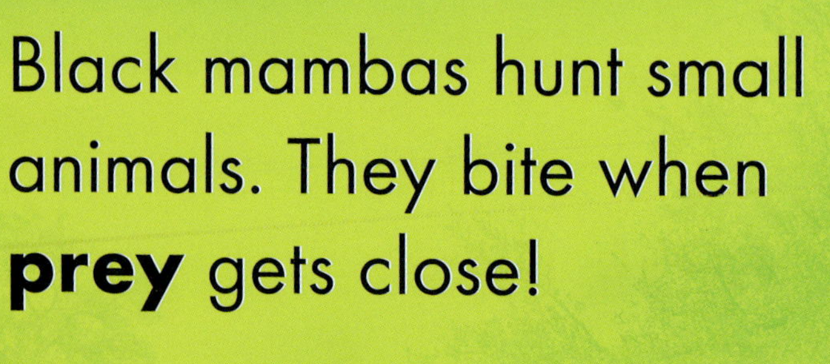

Black mambas hunt small animals. They bite when **prey** gets close!

Their **fangs** let out venom to stop prey. The snakes swallow their meals whole.

Black Mamba Food
mice
squirrels
small
birds

Black mambas are fast! They can move over 12 miles (19 kilometers) per hour.

Their speed often helps them escape **predators**.

Black mambas usually **flee** from predators. But sometimes, they fight back.

They flick their tongues and hiss.
If enemies get too close,
black mambas attack!

Growing Up Mamba

Female black mambas lay up to 25 eggs in a **burrow**. Then they leave.

Babies **hatch** two or three months later.

hatching

Baby black mambas take care of themselves as soon as they hatch. They grow quickly.

Soon, they rule their African home!

Black Mamba Stats
status in the wild: least concern
life span: around 11 years

Glossary

bask–to lay in the sun; cold-blooded animals often bask to raise their body temperatures.

burrow–a tunnel or hole that an animal uses for a home

fangs–long, sharp teeth

flee–to leave quickly

hatch–to break out of an egg

predators–animals that hunt other animals for food

prey–animals that are hunted by other animals for food

reptiles–cold-blooded animals that have backbones and lay eggs

savannas–flat grasslands with few trees

scales–plates that cover an animal's body

venom–poison produced by an animal, usually for hunting

To Learn More

AT THE LIBRARY

Boutland, Craig. *Black Mamba.* Minneapolis, Minn.: Bearport Publishing, 2021.

Culliford, Amy. *Black Mamba.* New York, N.Y.: Crabtree Publishing, 2022.

Levy, Janey. *Black Mamba vs. Blue-ringed Octopus.* New York, N.Y.: Gareth Stevens Publishing, 2022.

ON THE WEB

FACTSURFER

Factsurfer.com gives you a safe, fun way to find more information.

1. Go to www.factsurfer.com.
2. Enter "black mambas" into the search box and click 🔍.
3. Select your book cover to see a list of related content.

Index

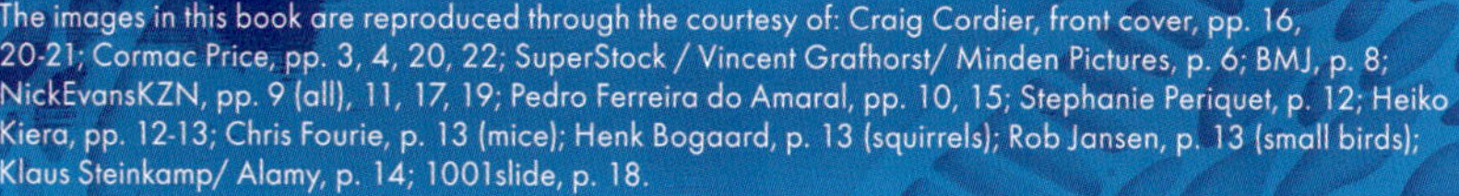
The images in this book are reproduced through the courtesy of: Craig Cordier, front cover, pp. 16, 20-21; Cormac Price, pp. 3, 4, 20, 22; SuperStock / Vincent Grafhorst/ Minden Pictures, p. 6; BMJ, p. 8; NickEvansKZN, pp. 9 (all), 11, 17, 19; Pedro Ferreira do Amaral, pp. 10, 15; Stephanie Periquet, p. 12; Heiko Kiera, pp. 12-13; Chris Fourie, p. 13 (mice); Henk Bogaard, p. 13 (squirrels); Rob Jansen, p. 13 (small birds); Klaus Steinkamp/ Alamy, p. 14; 1001slide, p. 18.